The California
Artichoke Cookbook

The California Artichoke Cookbook

FROM THE
California Artichoke Advisory Board

EDITED AND COMPILED BY
Mary Comfort, Noreen Griffee
and Charlene Walker

Celestial Arts
Berkeley, California

To everyone who enjoys
good food, and to all the
growers who make it happen.

Copyright © 1998 by the California Artichoke Advisory Board.
All rights reserved. Published in the United States by Celestial Arts, an
imprint of the Crown Publishing Group, a division of Random House, Inc.,
New York.

www.crownpublishing.com
www.tenspeed.com

Library of Congress Cataloging-in-Publication Data
The California artichoke cookbook / from the California Artichoke
Advisory Board ; edited and compiled by Mary Comfort, Noreen
Griffee, Charlene Walker.
    p.   cm
  1. Cookery (Artichoke) 2. Artichoke— California.   I. Comfort,
Mary.   II. Griffee, Noreen.   III. Walker, Charkene.   IV. California
Artichoke Advisory Board.
TX803.A7C35 1998
641.6′532—dc21   97-44106
                                                            CIP

ISBN-13: 978-0-89087-855-2 (alk. paper)

Printed in Malaysia
Cover photograph: California Artichoke Advisory Board
Cover design: Green Design
Interior design: Star Type

For more information about California artichokes, contact the
California Artichoke Advisory Board, P.O. Box 747, Castroville, CA 95012

Contents

Introduction   6

Artichoke Basics   8

Selecting the Best
How to Store
How to Prepare
How to Cook
How to Eat
Artichoke Nutrition

Sauces, Dips and Appetizers   17

Soups, Salads, Sautés and Sides   41

Brunch, Lunch and Dinner, Too   67

Conversions   96

Introduction

As one of the world's oldest known foods, artichokes enjoy a rich heritage and hold a special place in our history. First cultivated for food in the Mediterranean basin thousands of years ago, they remain a popular favorite throughout that part of the world to this day. The temperate climate is ideal for this hardy thistle and Italian, Greek, Turkish and Middle Eastern cuisines have inspired many classic artichoke dishes.

Artichokes traveled with Italian immigrants to the northern California coast during the late 1800s. Relatively mild, usually frost-free winters and cool, foggy summers proved to be perfect growing conditions. Today, virtually 100 percent of the U.S. supply of artichokes is grown in California with most of the crop coming from the central coastal region. In fact this prickly immigrant reigns supreme as "The Official Vegetable of Monterey County."

Whenever we eat an artichoke, we are actually eating a flower bud. As a perennial in the thistle group of the sunflower (Compositae) family, the artichoke bud, if allowed to blossom, would measure up to seven inches in diameter and be a beautiful purple-violet color with a fragrance much like lilac.

In full growth, the artichoke plant spreads to cover an area about six feet in diameter and reaches a height of three to four feet. Long, arching, serrated leaves give the mature plant a fern-like appearance.

California artichokes are available in most markets throughout the year. The peak season is the spring—March, April and May. They have a rich, meaty quality with a distinct nut-like flavor that makes them tremendously versatile and fun to eat!

Whether or not this is your first experience with an artichoke, we wish you good health and happy eating!

Artichoke Basics

Selecting The Best

Choose artichokes that are heavy for their size. Artichokes come in sizes ranging from "baby" to jumbo and all are mature when picked. Small or baby artichokes are ideal for marinating, sautéing or adding to your favorite stews and pot roasts. Medium sizes are perfect for salads, side dishes and light meals. When properly trimmed, they can be sliced and sautéed or added to stir-fry or pasta dishes. Serve the largest sizes as an appetizer with a dip or stuff them for a special entrée.

How To Store

An artichoke will look and taste fresh for up to one week if properly handled and stored. Do not wash before storing. To keep longer than several days, drizzle a few drops of water on each artichoke, place in a plastic bag, seal airtight and refrigerate. Cooked artichokes should be cooled completely, covered and refrigerated for up to one week.

How To Prepare

Wash the artichoke under cold, running water. To preserve its color, use only stainless steel knives for any cutting.

Immediately rub any cut surface with lemon juice or place artichoke in acidulated water. (Add 1 tablespoon vinegar or lemon juice per quart of water.) Acidulated water helps prevent discoloration of artichokes.

Whole Artichokes: Pull off the lower outer leaves of the artichokes. Cut the stem to 1 inch or less. If desired, cut off the top quarter and tips of the remaining leaves.

Artichoke Halves: Cut in half lengthwise and remove fuzzy centers.

Artichoke Quarters: Cut halves in half again.

(Remember to rub cut surfaces with lemon juice or place in acidulated water, as noted above.)

Artichoke Hearts: Use small or medium-sized artichokes. Bend back the outer leaves of the artichokes until they snap off easily near the base. The edible portion should remain on the artichoke. Continue to snap off and discard dark green leaves until the central core of pale green is reached. Cut off the top 2 inches of artichoke; discard. Cut the stem to 1 inch or less. Trim the outer dark green layer from the artichoke bottom. Remove fuzzy center; discard. *Place in acidulated water.*

Artichoke Heart Halves: Cut in half lengthwise. Remove the fuzzy centers. *Place in acidulated water.* For **Quarters** or **Wedges**, cut in half again or smaller. *Place in acidulated water.*

Artichoke Bottoms: Use large artichokes. Bend back the outer leaves of the artichokes until they snap off easily near the base. The edible portion should remain on the artichoke. Continue to snap off and discard the dark green leaves until the central core of pale green is reached. Cut off the stem and top leaves $\frac{1}{2}$ inch above the base of the leaves; discard. Trim the outer dark green layer from the artichoke bottom. Remove fuzzy center; discard. *Place in acidulated water.*

Baby Artichokes: Baby artichokes have no developed fuzz or fibrous leaves in the center. So, with careful trimming, you have a completely edible artichoke.

Bend back the outer leaves of the artichokes until they snap off easily near the base *(illustration 1)*. Continue until the pale green core is reached. Cut off the top point where pale green meets dark green *(illustration 2)*. Cut off the stem *(illustration 3)*. Trim the outer dark green layer from the base. *Place in acidulated water.*

Baby Artichoke Halves: Cut in half lengthwise *(illustration 4)*. Remove the pink or purple leaves and the fuzzy centers. If the interior is white, the entire artichoke is edible. *Place in acidulated water.*

How to Cook

Use stainless steel, enamel or other coated cookware. Do *not* use cast iron or aluminum cookware as they will turn the artichoke dark.

Boiling

In a deep saucepan or pot, stand the prepared artichokes in 3 inches of water. (If desired, add oil, lemon juice, and seasonings.) Cover and simmer 25 to 40 minutes, depending on size, or until the leaf near the center pulls out easily. Invert the artichoke to drain.

Steaming

Place the prepared artichokes on a rack over boiling water. Cover and steam 25 to 40 minutes, depending on size, or until the leaf near the center pulls out easily.

Microwaving (600–700 watt oven)

For one artichoke: Invert the prepared artichoke in a deep, microwave-safe 1-quart bowl. Add 2 tablespoons water. (If desired add oil, lemon juice, and seasonings.) Cover with plastic wrap; prick with a fork to allow steam to escape. Cook in microwave at HIGH (100%) 6 to 8 minutes. Rotate bowl one-half turn halfway through cooking time. Let stand, covered, 5 minutes. When done, the leaf near the center will pull out easily.

For four artichokes: Follow above procedure placing artichokes in 2½-quart bowl. Add 4 tablespoons water. Cook, covered, 12 to 14 minutes.

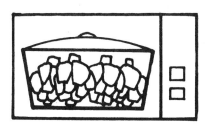

How to Eat

Cooked artichokes may be served hot or cold. To eat, pull off outer leaves one at a time.

Dip base of leaf into sauce or melted butter.

Pull through teeth to remove soft, tender base of the leaf. (Whether you hold the leaf right-side-up or upside-down is a matter of preference!) Discard remainder.

Continue until all leaves have been removed. When you reach the central cone of inner leaves, lift off and discard.

Spoon out fuzzy center at base; discard. The bottom, or heart, of the artichoke is entirely edible. Cut into small pieces and dip into sauce. Enjoy!

Artichoke Nutrition

Artichokes are a fun, healthy food for the entire family. Artichokes are a favorite food in their
native Mediterranean region, an area of the world
with one of the lowest rates of chronic disease and one
of the longest life expectancies. Mediterranean cuisine
features artichokes, other vegetables and fruits, and
little saturated fat.

Health professionals recommend a low fat diet with
at least *five* servings of fruit and vegetables a day to
reduce the risk of certain cancers, heart disease, obesity
and diabetes.

Artichokes are a healthy, low calorie, low sodium
food. They are fat free and have no cholesterol. An
average, 12-ounce artichoke is a good source of
vitamin C, folate, magnesium and potassium, and
contains *only* 25 calories.

Artichokes, the ultimate finger food,
are equally at home around the patio, at a picnic
or elegantly dressed for a party.
Dipping and artichokes go hand-in-hand.
Here you'll find the two most preferred dips —
melted butter and mayonnaise —
elevated to new culinary heights.
And we've included other ideas . . .
from the simple to the sublime.

Sauces, Dips and Appetizers

Classic Butter Sauce   18

Herbed Butter Sauce   19

Hollandaise Sauce   20

Vinaigrette • Honey Mustard Sauce   21

Dill Sauce • Blue Cheese Sauce   22

Creamy Caesar Dip • Dip with Zip!   23

Oriental Dipping Sauce   24

Sun-Dried Tomato Pesto   25

Tangy Mayonnaise   26

Ship Ahoy Dip   27

Queso-Chili Dip   28

Marinated Artichokes   29

Castroville French-Fried Artichokes   30

Shrimp Cocktail in Artichokes   32

Baked Artichoke Wedges   34

California Confetti Brie   35

Hummus-Filled Artichokes   36

Artichoke Aubergine   38

Classic Butter Sauce

1 cup melted butter
1/4 cup lemon juice
1/4 cup chopped parsley
1/4 teaspoon salt
1/2 teaspoon dry mustard

Combine all ingredients. Simmer 5 minutes. Serve warm.

Makes about 1 1/2 cups

Herbed Butter Sauce

1½ cups dry white wine
⅓ cup minced shallots
1 tablespoon lemon juice
1 teaspoon oregano, crushed
3 tablespoons butter, chilled
1 tablespoon minced parsley

Heat wine and shallots over medium heat until mixture
is reduced to ¾ cup. Add lemon juice and oregano.
Cool slightly; return pan to low heat. Slowly add butter
in small amounts, stirring constantly until sauce
thickens. Garnish with parsley. Serve warm.

Makes about 1 cup

Hollandaise Sauce

3 egg yolks
1/4 cup water
2 tablespoons lemon juice
1/2 cup firm cold butter, cut into eighths
1/8 teaspoon paprika
   dash ground red pepper

In small saucepan, heat together egg yolks, water and lemon juice. Cook over very low heat, stirring constantly, until yolk mixture bubbles at edges. Stir in butter, 1 piece at a time, until melted and sauce is thickened. Stir in paprika, red pepper and salt to taste. Remove from heat. Serve warm. Cover and chill if not used immediately.

Makes about 3/4 cup

Vinaigrette

- ⅓ cup olive oil
- 2 tablespoons balsamic vinegar
- 1 tablespoon sugar
- 1 tablespoon Dijon mustard
- ⅛ teaspoon garlic powder

Combine all ingredients; mix well.

Makes about ⅔ cup

Honey Mustard Sauce

- ¼ cup prepared mustard
- 2 tablespoons cider vinegar
- 2 tablespoons honey

Combine all ingredients; mix well.

Makes about ½ cup

Dill Sauce

1 cup plain yogurt
1/4 cup mayonnaise
3 tablespoons minced green onions
2 teaspoons chopped capers
3/4 teaspoon dried dill weed

Combine all ingredients; mix well.

Makes about 1 1/2 cups

Blue Cheese Sauce

1 package (8 ounces) cream cheese, softened
1/4 cup sour cream
2 tablespoons crumbled blue cheese
1/2 teaspoon Worcestershire sauce
1/8 teaspoon dry mustard

In a saucepan, stir together all ingredients. Over low heat, stir constantly until blended. Serve warm.

Makes 1 1/4 cups

Creamy Caesar Dip

1/3 cup mayonnaise

1/4 cup olive oil

2 tablespoons lemon juice

1 teaspoon Worcestershire sauce

1 teaspoon anchovy paste

1 clove garlic, minced

Combine all ingredients; mix well.

Makes 2/3 cup

Dip with Zip!

1/2 cup sour cream

1/2 cup mayonnaise

1 1/2 tablespoons chopped chives

1 tablespoon prepared horseradish

1/2 teaspoon salt

Combine all ingredients; mix well.

Makes 1 cup

Oriental
Dipping Sauce

1/4 cup firmly packed brown sugar
2 tablespoons cider vinegar
2 tablespoons soy sauce
1 teaspoon sesame oil
1/8 teaspoon ground ginger

Combine all ingredients; mix well.

Makes about 1/2 cup

Variation:

Creamy Thai Sauce: Blend 1/4 cup creamy peanut butter
with Oriental Dipping Sauce;
mix thoroughly.

Makes about 3/4 cup

Sun-Dried Tomato Pesto

1   jar (8.5 ounces) sun-dried tomatoes
1   clove garlic, minced
1   teaspoon dried basil, crushed
1/2   teaspoon dried oregano, crushed
1/8   teaspoon pepper
    salt to taste

Combine all ingredients into blender; blend until almost smooth.

Makes about 1 cup

Tangy Mayonnaise

1⅓ cups mayonnaise
¼ cup cider vinegar
2 tablespoons milk
1 tablespoon sugar
1 tablespoon grated onion
2 teaspoons prepared mustard
½ teaspoon ground celery seed
½ teaspoon salt
⅛ teaspoon pepper

Blend mayonnaise with all ingredients; mix well.

Makes about 1¾ cups

Variations:

Herb: Add ¼ teaspoon *each* tarragon and basil.

Aioli: Add 1 clove garlic, minced.

Caper: Add 2 tablespoons capers, drained and chopped.

Ship Ahoy Dip

 1   can (6½ ounces) minced clams
 2   tablespoons clam juice
 3   ounces cream cheese, softened
 1   teaspoon lemon juice
¼   teaspoon garlic salt

Drain clams, reserving 2 tablespoons clam juice. Blend clam juice with cream cheese, lemon juice and garlic salt; mix well. Stir in clams. Refrigerate until ready to serve.

Makes about ¾ cup

Queso-Chili Dip

2 packages (8 ounces *each*) cream cheese, softened
1 can (7 1/2 or 8 ounces) stewed tomatoes
1 can (4 ounces) diced green chiles, drained
1 tablespoon chopped onion
1/4 teaspoon hot pepper sauce
1/8 teaspoon salt

Blend cream cheese with mixer until smooth. Fold in remaining ingredients.

Makes about 2 1/2 cups

Marinated Artichokes

24 California baby artichokes
3 quarts water
2 cups white vinegar
3 cloves garlic
1 teaspoon salt
1 cup *each* wine vinegar and vegetable oil
1/2 teaspoon garlic powder
3 tablespoons minced parsley

Prepare artichokes as directed for **Baby Artichokes** (see page 11). Bring water, white vinegar, garlic and salt to a rolling boil. Stir in artichokes. Continue stirring for one minute. Cover and boil 10 to 15 minutes or until tender. Drain and cool. Cut artichokes into halves or quarters, depending on size. Remove any purple leaves. Mix together wine vinegar, oil, garlic powder and parsley. Add artichokes. Stir, cover and refrigerate. These taste better on the second day and will keep several weeks in the refrigerator; stir occasionally.

Makes 6 servings

Castroville
French-Fried Artichokes

4 medium California artichokes
1 egg
½ cup milk
½ cup biscuit baking mix
¼ cup flour
1½ teaspoons baking powder
1 teaspoon salt
½ teaspoon garlic powder
¼ cup finely chopped onion
1 tablespoon chopped parsley
   oil for deep-fat frying

Prepare artichokes as directed for **Artichoke Hearts** (see page 10) and cut into thin wedges. In small bowl, blend together egg and milk. Stir in biscuit baking mix, flour, baking powder, salt and garlic powder until well mixed. Fold in onion and parsley. Dip artichoke wedges in batter to thinly coat. In deep-fat fryer or large saucepan, heat 2 inches of oil to 350° F on deep-fat thermometer. Fry artichokes, a few at a time, until

golden brown, about 6 to 8 minutes.
With slotted spoon remove artichokes and
drain well on paper towels. Sprinkle with salt,
if desired. Serve hot.

Makes about 8 servings

───────

*Castroville, California, was founded by
Juan Bautista Castro in 1863. Today, nearly two-thirds
of the State's artichoke acreage is located nearby.
Two major artichoke packers are located here along with
the nation's only artichoke processing plant.
Is it any wonder that the townspeople have proclaimed
Castroville as the "Artichoke Center of the World"?*

───────

Shrimp Cocktail
in Artichokes

4 medium California artichokes
   Cocktail Sauce (recipe follows)
1 medium avocado, peeled and diced
2 tablespoons lemon juice
¾ cup cooked, shelled small fresh shrimp
   parsley sprigs, optional
   lemon wedges

Prepare and cook artichokes as directed for **Whole Artichokes** (see page 9). Remove center petals and fuzzy center from artichokes. Spoon 1 tablespoon Cocktail Sauce into center of each artichoke. Toss avocado with lemon juice until well-coated; drain. Combine avocado and shrimp; spoon into artichokes. Top each with 1 tablespoon Cocktail Sauce. Garnish with parsley and lemon wedges. Pass remaining Cocktail Sauce as dip for leaves. Serve immediately.

Makes 4 servings

Cocktail Sauce: Combine $\frac{2}{3}$ cup *each* chili sauce and ketchup, 4 teaspoons prepared horseradish and 1 tablespoon lemon juice; mix well. Chill.

Makes $1\frac{1}{2}$ cups sauce

Baked Artichoke Wedges

      1 large California artichoke
      1 egg
      1 tablespoon water
      1 teaspoon Dijon mustard
    1/2 cup fine dry bread crumbs *or* cornmeal
    1/8 teaspoon *each* pepper and paprika
         dash salt
      3 tablespoons butter *or* margarine

Prepare artichokes as directed for **Artichoke Hearts** (see page 10) and cut into thin wedges. Combine egg, water and mustard. Combine bread crumbs, pepper, paprika and salt. Dip artichoke wedges into egg mixture, then into crumb mixture. Melt butter in 15 × 10 × 3/4-inch baking pan. Place artichoke wedges in pan; turn to coat both sides with butter. Bake at 425° F for 15 to 20 minutes or until golden.

Makes about 24 to 30 appetizers

California
Confetti Brie

8	small California artichokes
1/4	cup minced onion
2	tablespoons olive oil
1/4	cup dry white wine
1	cup milk
2	teaspoons cornstarch
4 to 5	ounces Brie cheese, rind removed and cheese cubed
1/4	cup chopped red bell pepper
1	tablespoon capers

Prepare and cook artichokes as directed for **Whole Artichokes** (see page 9). Sauté onion in oil until translucent; stir in wine and heat 1 minute. Combine milk and cornstarch; stir into wine mixture and cook 2 minutes or until thickened. Stir in cheese, one cube at a time, over low heat until smooth. Stir in red pepper and capers. Spoon a portion of cheese mixture onto each serving plate; arrange artichoke in center.

Makes 8 servings

Hummus-Filled Artichokes

4 large California artichokes
1²⁄₃ cups drained, cooked *or* canned
garbanzo beans (chick peas)
¹⁄₄ cup water
¹⁄₄ cup toasted sesame seeds
3 tablespoons lemon juice
2 tablespoons olive oil
1 clove garlic, minced
dash bottled hot pepper sauce
¹⁄₂ teaspoon grated lemon peel
salt and pepper
parsley sprigs
whole wheat pita bread

Prepare and cook artichokes as directed for **Whole Artichokes** (see page 9). Reserve a few garbanzos for garnish. Combine remaining garbanzos in food processor or blender with water, sesame seeds, lemon juice, olive oil, garlic, hot pepper sauce and grated lemon peel. Blend until smooth and of thick dipping consistency. Salt and pepper to taste. Remove center

petals and fuzzy centers of cooked artichokes; discard. Fill centers of artichokes
with garbanzo mixture. Garnish with reserved
garbanzos and parsley. Serve with whole wheat
pita bread.

Makes 4 servings.

Hummus *is a Middle Eastern thick sauce traditionally
served with pita bread. It is made from mashed garbanzo
beans (also called chick peas) and seasoned with lemon
juice, garlic and olive oil.*

Artichoke Aubergine

4 large California artichokes
¾ cup sun-dried tomatoes
    (not oil-packed)
1 small eggplant, peeled and diced
2 cups chicken broth
¼ cup chopped onion
1 tablespoon *each* chopped fresh oregano and
    basil *or* 1 teaspoon *each* dried oregano
    and basil, crushed
1 to 2 cloves garlic, minced
¼ teaspoon salt
¼ teaspoon pepper

Prepare and cook artichokes as directed for **Whole Artichokes** (see page 9). Halve artichokes lengthwise; remove center petals and fuzzy centers of artichokes. Remove outer leaves of artichokes; reserve. Trim out hearts and chop finely. Set aside. Cover tomatoes with boiling water; let set for 3 minutes or until softened. Drain and rinse; chop. Cook eggplant in simmering chicken broth for 10 minutes; drain well. In blender or food processor, place chopped tomatoes, drained

eggplant, onion, herbs, garlic, salt and
pepper. Cover and process until nearly
smooth. Taste for seasoning. Stir in chopped
artichoke hearts. Serve artichoke leaves with dip.

Makes 2 cups

October through February brings
"winter-kissed" artichokes that have been touched by frost
and browned on their outer leaves. But don't be fooled —
these are just as tender and tasty inside as
their spring counterparts.

Soups, Salads, Sautés and Sides

Artichoke Shrimp Bisque   42

Spring Soup   44

Cream of Artichoke Soup   46

Artichoke with Smoked Salmon Pasta Salad   47

Stuffed Artichoke with Bulgur and Gorgonzola   48

California Wild Rice and Artichoke Salad   50

Artichoke Halves with Vinaigrette   52

Warm Artichoke and Scallop Salad   53

Tarragon Artichoke Sauté   54

Roman-Style Artichokes   55

Artichoke Sauté with Mustard and Chives   56

Stuffed Artichokes Southern-Style   57

Italian-Stuffed Artichokes   58

Baked Artichoke Casserole   59

Couscous-Stuffed Artichokes   60

Potato and Artichoke au Gratin   62

Risotto with Artichokes   64

Artichoke
Shrimp Bisque

6 large California artichokes
6 cups vegetable broth
2 pounds fresh *or* frozen shelled and
    deveined shrimp
1/3 cup chopped green onions
2 tablespoons instant minced onion
1 teaspoon onion salt
1/8 teaspoon pepper
2 cups heavy cream
2/3 cup flour
2 egg yolks, slightly beaten
1 can (1 pound) small whole
    carrots, undrained

Prepare and cook artichokes as directed for **Whole Artichokes** (see page 9). Scrape meat from artichoke leaves; reserve. Remove and discard fuzzy centers. Place artichoke bottoms and reserved meat from leaves in blender; process until smooth. Heat broth to boiling. Add shrimp, green onions, onion, onion salt and pepper and cook 10 minutes or until shrimp are tender. Add

artichoke purée and cook 5 minutes.
Add cream to flour and blend; beat in egg
yolks. Stir cream mixture into artichoke mixture and cook over low heat, stirring constantly,
until thickened. Add carrots and heat to serving
temperature.

Makes 10 to 12 servings

Spring Soup

2 large California artichokes
6 cups chicken broth
1 small sweet potato *or* carrot, very thinly
   sliced
1 cup thinly sliced mushrooms
1 cup slivered, cooked chicken
   salt and pepper
1 cup shredded spinach leaves
   Omelet Garnish (recipe follows)

Prepare artichokes as directed for **Artichoke Hearts** (see page 10) and cut into thin wedges. Bring chicken broth to boil in saucepan. Add artichokes, sweet potato and mushrooms; cook gently 10 minutes or until vegetables are barely tender. Add chicken; salt and pepper to taste. Place spinach in individual bowls. Ladle hot soup over; top with Omelet Garnish.

Makes about 6 servings

Omelet Garnish: Beat together 2 eggs,
1 tablespoon water and a dash of salt.
Heat lightly oiled small skillet. Pour in egg
mixture; sprinkle with 2 tablespoons grated
Parmesan cheese. Cook until set but moist.
Remove and cool. Roll loosely; cut into slivers.

Makes ¾ cup

Cream of Artichoke Soup

2 large California artichokes
1 can (10½ ounces) condensed chicken broth
2 tablespoons lemon juice
¼ cup chopped onion
¼ teaspoon dried thyme leaves
⅛ teaspoon pepper
1 cup light cream

Prepare artichokes as directed for **Whole Artichokes** (see page 9) and cut into quarters, removing center petals and fuzzy centers; discard. In 3½ quart saucepan combine artichokes, chicken broth, lemon juice, 1 cup water, onion, thyme and pepper. Bring to boiling; reduce heat and simmer, covered, for 30 minutes or until artichokes are tender. Remove artichokes, reserving liquid. Remove leaves and scrape meat; reserve. Cut artichoke hearts into pieces. In blender, combine *strained* cooking liquid, the artichoke meat, hearts and cream. Blend at high speed for 2 minutes. Refrigerate overnight. Serve warm or chilled.

Makes 4 servings

Artichoke with Smoked Salmon Pasta Salad

4   medium California artichokes
8   ounces orzo-style pasta
$^1/_2$ cup *each* plain yogurt and mayonnaise
$^1/_4$ cup chopped fresh dill
4   teaspoons Dijon mustard
4   ounces smoked salmon, flaked
    salt and pepper to taste
    fresh dill to garnish

Prepare and cook artichokes as directed for **Whole Artichokes** (see page 9). Cut artichokes in half and remove center petals and fuzzy centers; discard. Cook orzo according to package directions. Combine yogurt, mayonnaise, dill and mustard; add to cooked and drained orzo and mix well. Gently stir in smoked salmon; season with salt and pepper. Fill centers of prepared artichokes with pasta mixture. Garnish with a sprig of fresh dill.

Makes 4 servings

Stuffed Artichoke with Bulgur and Gorgonzola

6	large California artichokes
2	cups bulgur
	Herb Dressing (recipe follows)
1½	cups cooked garbanzo beans (chick peas)
¼	cup chopped walnuts, toasted
1	red bell pepper, chopped
¼	cup crumbled Gorgonzola cheese

Prepare and cook artichokes as directed for **Whole Artichokes** (see page 9), adding juice of 1 lemon and clove of garlic while cooking. Cover bulgur with boiling water. Let stand 30 minutes; drain. When bulgur is cool, toss with Herb Dressing, garbanzo beans, walnuts, red pepper and cheese. Remove center petals and fuzzy centers of cooked artichokes. Fill centers of artichokes with bulgur mixture.

Makes 6 servings

Herb Dressing: Combine $\frac{1}{2}$ cup lemon juice, 1 tablespoon *each* chopped fresh tarragon and chervil, 2 teaspoons finely chopped onion, 1 clove garlic, minced, $\frac{1}{2}$ teaspoon sugar, $\frac{1}{4}$ teaspoon dry mustard and salt and pepper to taste. Blend in $\frac{3}{4}$ cup olive oil; mix well.

Makes about 1 $\frac{1}{4}$ cups

California Wild Rice and Artichoke Salad

4	medium California artichokes
2	cups cooked wild rice
I	cup cooked white rice
1/4	cup golden raisins
1/4	cup dried apricots, slivered
1/4	cup canned pineapple tidbits
1/4	cup sliced almonds, toasted
1/4	cup chopped fresh mint
4	green onions, thinly sliced
1/2	teaspoon grated orange peel
I	tablespoon orange juice
I	teaspoon salt
1/4	teaspoon white pepper
	Curry Dressing (recipe follows)

Prepare and cook artichokes as directed for **Whole Artichokes** (see page 9). Cook wild rice and white rice separately, according to package directions. Drain wild rice, if necessary. Combine rices in large mixing bowl; cool completely. Add raisins, apricots, pineapple, almonds, mint, green onions, orange peel, orange juice, salt and pepper. Prepare Curry Dressing. Remove center petals and fuzzy centers of cooked artichokes. Fill center of artichokes with rice mixture. Serve with Curry Dressing.

Makes 4 servings

Curry Dressing: Combine 2 cups mayonnaise with 2 tablespoons *each* lemon juice and soy sauce, 1 tablespoon *each* curry powder and coarsely chopped chutney.

Makes about 2¹/₃ cups

Artichoke Halves with Vinaigrette

2 large California artichokes
⅓ cup coarsely chopped walnuts, toasted
Vinaigrette Dressing (recipe follows)
blue cheese
lemon or lime wedges

Prepare and cook artichokes as directed for **Whole Artichokes** (see page 9). Cut artichokes in half and remove center petals and fuzzy centers; discard. Arrange on salad plates, drizzle with Vinaigrette Dressing and add walnuts. Top with a thin wedge of blue cheese and lemon, if desired. Serve remaining dressing on the side.

Makes 4 servings

Vinaigrette Dressing: Combine 1 cup olive or other vegetable oil with ¼ cup balsamic vinegar. Add 1 teaspoon Dijon mustard; salt and pepper to taste. Blend well.

Makes 1¼ cups

Warm Artichoke and Scallop Salad

    2   large California artichokes
   12   ounces bay scallops
   1/2 cup lime juice
    2   tablespoons chopped cilantro
    1   tablespoon olive oil
    2   teaspoons sugar
    1   teaspoon cornstarch
    3   drops hot pepper sauce
   1/2 cup grated Swiss cheese

Prepare and cook artichokes as directed for **Whole Artichokes** (see page 9). Cut artichokes in half and remove center petals and fuzzy centers. Combine scallops, lime juice and cilantro; marinate 10 minutes. Remove scallops from marinade, reserving marinade. Sauté scallops in olive oil. Blend sugar, cornstarch and hot pepper sauce into reserved marinade and add to skillet. Heat until thickened. Arrange scallops and sauce on each artichoke half. Garnish with cheese. Place under broiler just until cheese starts to melt. Serve immediately.

Makes 4 servings

Tarragon Artichoke Sauté

2 large California artichokes
1 small onion, cut into wedges
1 medium carrot, thinly sliced diagonally
1 tablespoon olive oil
1 cup sliced mushrooms
½ cup dairy sour cream
1 teaspoon flour
2 teaspoons fresh chopped tarragon *or*
    ½ teaspoon dried tarragon, crushed
¼ teaspoon grated lemon peel (optional)
    salt and pepper to taste

Prepare artichokes as directed for **Artichoke Hearts** (see page 10) and cut into thin wedges. Sauté artichokes, onion and carrot in olive oil over medium heat for about 8 to 10 minutes or until tender. Add mushrooms; cover and cook 2 minutes. Combine sour cream, flour, tarragon, lemon peel, salt and pepper; stir into artichoke mixture. Bring mixture to simmering; reduce heat to low and cook 2 minutes more (do not boil).

Makes 4 servings

Roman-Style Artichokes

12 to 18 California baby artichokes
1 onion, coarsely chopped
1 clove garlic, chopped
¼ cup olive oil
1 cup chicken broth
½ teaspoon *each* dried basil
and marjoram
salt and pepper

Prepare artichokes as directed for **Baby Artichokes** (see page 11), cut into halves. Sauté artichokes, onion and garlic in olive oil until golden. Add broth, basil and marjoram. Cover and bring to a boil over high heat. Reduce to low and simmer, covered, 10 to 15 minutes or until tender. Salt and pepper to taste.

Makes 4 servings

Artichoke Sauté with Mustard and Chives

24 California baby artichokes
1/2 cup chopped natural almonds
1 tablespoon olive oil
1/4 cup butter *or* margarine
2 tablespoons Dijon mustard
1 tablespoon lemon juice
2 tablespoons chopped fresh parsley
2 tablespoons finely sliced chives
1/2 teaspoon salt
1/4 teaspoon freshly ground white pepper

Prepare artichokes as directed for **Baby Artichokes** (see page 11), and cut into quarters. Sauté almonds in oil until golden; reserve. Sauté artichokes in butter 10 to 15 minutes or until tender. Add mustard and lemon juice and sauté 1 minute longer. Toss with almonds, parsley, chives and salt and pepper.

Makes 6 servings

Stuffed Artichokes
Southern-Style

6 large California artichokes
¾ cup chopped celery
¼ cup chopped onion
1 clove garlic, minced
¼ cup butter *or* margarine
2 cups cornbread dressing mix
¼ cup chopped parsley
½ cup chicken broth
½ cup chopped pecans, toasted

Prepare and cook artichokes as directed for **Whole Artichokes** (see page 9). Sauté celery, onion and garlic in butter until vegetables are tender. Remove from heat; stir in dressing mix, parsley, chicken broth and pecans. Remove center petals and fuzzy centers of cooked artichokes. Fill centers with dressing mixture. Bake at 375° F for 15 minutes or until thoroughly heated.

Makes 6 servings

Italian-Stuffed Artichokes

        4 large California artichokes
    1 1/2 cups seasoned bread crumbs
      1/2 cup grated Parmesan cheese
        1 large tomato, stemmed, seeded and chopped
        2 tablespoons chopped parsley
           olive oil
           lemon juice

Prepare artichokes as directed for **Whole Artichokes** (see page 9). Mix bread crumbs, Parmesan cheese, tomato and parsley together, using a little olive oil to moisten. Stuff filling between leaves of artichokes working from the outside to the center until leaves are too tight to be filled. Place the artichokes in a pot filled with about 1/2 inch of water. (The pot should be just large enough to hold the artichokes so that they touch.) Pour a little olive oil and lemon juice over the artichokes.

Bring the water to a boil, then reduce to a simmer and cover. Cook for approximately 1 hour or until center leaf pulls out easily.

Makes 4 servings

Baked Artichoke Casserole

2 medium California artichokes
2 medium onions, sliced thick
2 tablespoons olive oil
1 teaspoon Italian herb seasoning
2 medium tomatoes, sliced
6 ounces Mozzarella *or* Monterey Jack
cheese, sliced

Prepare artichokes as directed for **Artichoke Bottoms** (see page 10). Slice into $1/4$-inch thick rounds. Sauté onions in olive oil 5 to 8 minutes or until tender. Spoon evenly into 2-quart oven-proof baking dish. Sprinkle with Italian herb seasoning. Arrange tomato slices, artichoke slices and cheese slices on onions, over-lapping slightly in center of dish. Cover dish with lid or foil. Bake at 375° F for 40 minutes.

Makes 4 servings

Couscous-Stuffed Artichokes

4 large California artichokes
1½ cups chicken broth
1 teaspoon curry powder
¾ teaspoon ground cumin
½ teaspoon garlic salt
1 cup instant couscous
¼ cup currants
½ cup sliced green onions
½ cup slivered almonds, toasted and chopped
½ teaspoon grated lemon peel
2 tablespoons lemon juice
2 tablespoons vegetable oil
plain lowfat yogurt (optional)

Prepare and cook artichokes as directed for **Whole Artichokes** (see page 9). In medium saucepan combine chicken broth, curry powder, cumin and garlic salt; bring to a boil. Remove from heat; stir in couscous and currants. Cover and let stand 5 minutes. Fluff couscous with a fork. Stir in green onions and almonds. Combine lemon peel, lemon juice and vegetable oil; stir into couscous.

Remove center petals and fuzzy centers of cooked artichokes. Fill centers of artichokes with couscous mixture. Serve with plain yogurt, if desired.

Makes 4 generous servings

North African cuisine features a granular semolina called couscous. It's simple to prepare and a nice change from rice.

Potato and Artichoke au Gratin

3 medium California artichokes
2 tablespoons olive oil, *divided*
3 medium potatoes, thinly sliced
2 large garlic cloves, minced
2 teaspoons thyme, crushed
¾ teaspoon salt
¼ teaspoon pepper
½ cup *hot* chicken broth
½ cup soft bread crumbs

Prepare artichokes as directed for **Artichoke Hearts** (see page 10) and cut into thin wedges. Place 1 tablespoon

olive oil into 2 ½ quart baking dish.
Layer one third of potato slices into baking
dish. Top with half of the artichoke wedges.
Combine garlic, thyme, salt and pepper. Sprinkle
1 heaping teaspoon mixture over artichokes.
Layer with second third of potato slices, remaining
artichoke wedges, remaining seasonings and last third
of potato slices. Pour hot chicken broth evenly over
surface; sprinkle with bread crumbs and drizzle with
remaining 1 tablespoon olive oil. Cover dish with lid
or foil. Bake at 400° F for 30 minutes. Remove lid
or foil and continue baking 30 to 45 minutes longer or
until potatoes and artichokes are tender.

Makes 4 servings

Risotto with Artichokes

4 medium California artichokes
3 tablespoons olive oil
4 tablespoons butter, *divided*
6 tablespoons water
5 cups chicken broth
1½ cups arborio rice
1 cup grated Parmesan cheese, *divided*
salt and pepper, to taste

Prepare artichokes as directed for **Artichoke Hearts** (see page 10) and cut into eighths. Sauté artichokes in olive oil and 2 tablespoons butter until golden, about 5 minutes. Pour water over artichokes; cook, covered, until just tender, about 10 minutes; reserve in saucepan; keep warm. In a separate saucepan, bring chicken broth to a boil. Reduce heat to very low. Stir in rice and artichokes; cook, stirring constantly, 3 minutes. Add ⅓ cup hot broth, stirring frequently, until rice absorbs liquid. Repeat until all broth is used and rice is tender. If rice is not tender when stock is used up, add boiling water a

few tablespoons at a time, stirring constantly, until rice is tender. Stir in remaining 2 tablespoons butter and 3 tablespoons
Parmesan cheese. Season with salt and pepper.
Serve immediately. Pass remaining Parmesan cheese
at the table.

Makes 4 to 6 servings

———————

Risotto, *a creamy, slowly cooked rice dish,*
and artichokes probably joined forces in Lombardy,
the Italian province where Milan is located.
Both ingredients are commonly used
in Northern Italian cuisine.

———————

*Artichokes are a sure sign of spring
and with the season comes an abundance of festive
brunches, social luncheons and special dinners.
Discover the versatility of the amazing
artichoke for every meal occasion.*

Brunch, Lunch and Dinner, Too

Artichoke Quiche 68

Artichoke Benedict 70

Mushroom and Ham-Stuffed Artichokes 71

Artichoke Frittata 72

Hot Crab Salad in Artichokes 74

Artichokes del Mar 76

Artichoke and Angel Hair Pasta au Gratin 77

Country French Bake 78

Baby Artichoke Chicken Sauté 80

Pork and Artichoke Stew 82

Pork Chops Dijonnaise 84

Lamb and Bulgur-Filled Artichokes 86

Chicken Jerusalem 88

Fettuccine with Artichokes, Parmesan
and Sausage 90

Artichokes with Sweet Italian Sausage 92

Pasta with Sautéed Artichokes 94

Cypress Point Seafood Spectacular 95

Artichoke Quiche

3   medium California artichokes *or* 12 baby
     artichokes prepared as directed and
     cut into quarters
2   tablespoons butter
1   medium onion, chopped
1   clove garlic, minced
1/2 cup sour cream
4   eggs
1/2 cup half-and-half
2   cups shredded Swiss cheese
2   tablespoons chopped fresh parsley
1   teaspoon salt
1/8 teaspoon pepper
1/4 cup chopped ham (optional)
1   unbaked (9-inch) pie shell

Prepare artichokes as directed for **Artichoke Hearts**
or **Baby Artichokes** (see page 10 or 11) and cut into thin
wedges. Melt the butter and sauté artichoke wedges,
onion and garlic until tender. Combine sour cream, eggs
and half-and-half; mix until well blended. Add shredded
Swiss cheese, parsley, salt and pepper. Add ham if

68

desired. Mix thoroughly and pour into pie shell. Bake in preheated 425° F oven for 15 minutes. Reduce temperature to 350° F and cook for about 25 minutes or until set. Cool for about 25 minutes before serving.

Makes 8 servings

Artichoke Benedict

4   medium California artichokes
4   slices (¼-inch thick) Canadian bacon
4   eggs
    Hollandaise Sauce (see page 20)

Prepare and cook artichokes as directed for **Whole Artichokes** (see page 9). Brown Canadian bacon slices in skillet. Poach eggs in boiling, salted water. Spread leaves of artichokes open like flower petals. Remove center petals and fuzzy centers from artichokes and discard. Place bacon slices into artichoke centers, covering bottom, and top with poached eggs. Spoon on Hollandaise Sauce and serve immediately.

Makes 4 servings

Mushroom and
Ham-Stuffed Artichokes

4	medium California artichokes
1	cup chopped fresh mushrooms
1/3	cup chopped onion
2	tablespoons butter *or* margarine
1/2	pound cooked ham, chopped
1/4	cup chopped parsley
2	tablespoons flour
1/2	cup chicken broth
2	tablespoons dry sherry (optional)
	pepper
1	tablespoon olive oil

Prepare and cook artichokes as directed for **Whole Artichokes** (see page 9). Sauté mushrooms and onion in butter 5 minutes. Add ham and parsley; cook 5 minutes longer. Stir in flour. Gradually add broth; cook and stir until thickened. Add sherry and pepper to taste; mix well. Cool. Remove center petals and fuzzy centers of artichokes. Fill artichokes with ham mixture. Pour oil into a deep baking dish. Arrange artichokes in dish. Cover with foil and bake at 350° F for 30 minutes.

Makes 4 servings

Artichoke Frittata

8 California baby artichokes
1/2 pound angel hair pasta
3 tablespoons olive oil, *divided*
3 eggs, beaten
2 cups heavy whipping cream
1/4 cup grated Parmesan cheese
1 tablespoon fresh basil, chopped *or*
    1 teaspoon dried basil, crushed
1 clove garlic, minced
    salt and pepper
1 medium tomato, chopped
1/2 cup sautéed mixed mushrooms

Prepare and cook artichokes as directed for **Baby Artichokes** (see page 11), adding juice of 1 lemon, 1 carrot, coarsely chopped, 1 stalk celery, coarsely chopped, and 4 peppercorns while cooking. Cook pasta in boiling water until *al dente*; rinse in cold water and drain. Toss with 1 tablespoon olive oil; set aside. Beat eggs with heavy cream, Parmesan cheese, basil, garlic, salt and pepper. Cut artichokes in half; add to egg mixture with pasta, tomato and sautéed mushrooms. Heat remaining 2 tablespoons olive oil in large skillet. Pour in egg mixture. Cook on one side until golden brown and turn to brown second side. Cut into 4 wedges.

Makes 4 servings

Hot Crab Salad
in Artichokes

4 medium California artichokes
2 tablespoons butter *or* margarine
1/4 cup chopped green onions
1 can (10 3/4 ounces) condensed cream of
   celery soup, undiluted
1/2 cup sour cream
1 tablespoon dry sherry
1/8 teaspoon tarragon leaves, crushed
   dash white pepper
2 packages (6 ounces *each*) frozen crab meat,
   thawed and drained
1/2 cup diced water chestnuts

Prepare and cook artichokes as directed for **Whole Artichokes** (see page 9). Keep warm. In large skillet, melt butter. Add green onions; sauté until tender about 2 minutes. Stir in soup, sour cream, sherry, tarragon and white pepper. Cook, stirring constantly, for 5 minutes. Remove 1 cup mixture and set aside; keep warm.

Stir crab and water chestnuts into remaining mixture in skillet and cook until heated through. Remove center petals and fuzzy centers from artichokes; discard. Fill artichokes with crab mixture. Serve immediately with reserved sauce.

Makes 4 servings

Artichokes del Mar

3 medium California artichokes
1/4 cup clam juice
4 teaspoons cornstarch
1/8 teaspoon white pepper
   salt, to taste
1 cup half-and-half
2 tablespoons dry sherry
6 ounces *each* baby shrimp and bay scallops
1 tablespoon chopped parsley

Prepare and cook artichokes as directed for **Whole Artichokes** (see page 9). Halve artichokes and remove center petals and fuzzy centers; discard. Arrange halves on serving platter and keep warm. Combine clam juice, cornstarch, pepper and salt; stir in half-and-half. Cook and stir over medium heat until thickened. Add sherry, shrimp and scallops; cook and stir until thoroughly heated. Spoon seafood mixture into centers of artichokes. Sprinkle with parsley.

Makes 6 servings

Artichoke and Angel Hair Pasta au Gratin

3 large California artichokes
1 cup *each* red and yellow bell pepper,
  cut into ¼-inch strips
1 tablespoon olive oil
1 cup heavy cream
½ cup chicken broth
  salt and pepper, to taste
9 ounces hot, cooked fresh angel hair pasta,
  drained
4 ounces *each* Muenster and Cheddar
  cheeses, shredded

Prepare artichokes as directed for **Artichoke Hearts** (see page 10) and cut into wedges. Sauté artichoke wedges and peppers in olive oil about 5 minutes or until barely tender. Stir in cream, chicken broth, salt and pepper. Place pasta in bottom of 3-quart baking dish; spoon artichoke mixture over top. Combine cheeses; sprinkle over artichoke mixture. Bake at 375° F for 10 minutes. Place under broiler 30 to 45 seconds or until top is golden.

Makes 4 servings

Country French Bake

6	medium California artichokes
2½	pounds frying chicken pieces
	butter *or* margarine
4	carrots, cut into julienne strips
⅓	cup sliced green onions
¼	pound mushrooms, sliced
1	teaspoon salt
¼	teaspoon *each* pepper and thyme, crushed
1	cup *each* water and dry white wine
4	tablespoons cornstarch
2	cups chicken broth

Prepare and cook artichokes as directed for **Whole Artichokes** (see page 9). Cut into quarters, remove center petals and fuzzy centers from cooked artichokes. Brown chicken on both sides in 4 tablespoons butter in large skillet. Cover skillet and steam chicken for about 10 minutes. Remove chicken and set aside. If necessary, add 2 tablespoons additional butter to the skillet; add carrots and cook, uncovered, 5 minutes. Add green onions, mushrooms, salt, pepper and thyme to carrots; sauté 1 minute. Remove vegetables with slotted spoon and set aside. Stir water and wine into cornstarch. Add cornstarch mixture and broth to skillet and cook, stirring occasionally, until mixture is clear and thickened. Arrange artichokes, chicken pieces and sautéed vegetables in large roasting pan. Pour broth mixture over all. Cover tightly and bake in 375° F for 1 hour, or until chicken is tender, basting occasionally.

Makes 6 servings

Baby Artichoke
Chicken Sauté

16 California baby artichokes

¼ cup olive oil

4 half chicken breasts, skinned, boned and cut
    into chunks

2 red *or* yellow onions, sliced thick

4 cloves garlic, minced

1 tablespoon *each* chopped fresh basil
    and rosemary *or* 1 teaspoon *each*
    dried basil and rosemary, crushed

½ cup chicken broth

1 pound fettuccine, cooked and drained

Prepare artichokes as directed for **Baby Artichokes** (see page 11); cut into halves. Brown chicken in large skillet with 2 table-spoons oil; remove from pan and set aside. Add remaining 2 tablespoons oil and sauté onions until tender. Add artichokes to skillet with garlic, basil and rosemary. Cook until artichokes are tender, about 5 minutes. Stir in browned chicken and drizzle with chicken broth; heat through. Salt and pepper to taste, if desired. Serve over hot fettuccine.

Makes 4 servings

Pork and Artichoke Stew

3   medium California artichokes

1½   pounds boneless pork, cut into
      2-inch cubes

    oil

2   large onions, thinly sliced

1   clove garlic, minced

3   tablespoons flour

¼   teaspoon salt

⅛   teaspoon pepper

12   ounces beer

½   teaspoon thyme, crushed

3   peeled carrots, cut into 2-inch pieces

1   cup peeled, chopped tomatoes

Prepare artichokes as directed for **Artichoke Hearts** (see page 10) and cut into quarters. Brown pork thoroughly in 2 tablespoons oil in skillet; remove pork from skillet. Add 1 tablespoon oil if necessary; sauté onions and garlic until softened. Add flour, salt and pepper; cook and stir 2 minutes. Add beer and thyme; cook, stirring occasionally for 10 minutes. Layer pork, carrots,

tomatoes, artichokes and onion mixture
in 3-quart casserole. Bake, covered, at
350° F for 1½ hours or until pork is tender
and vegetables are cooked.

Makes 6 servings

▬▬▬▬▬

*The rich taste of stews, cassoulets and pot roasts benefit
from the addition of artichokes. Prepare artichokes
accordingly and simmer along with the other vegetables.*

▬▬▬▬▬

Pork Chops
Dijonnaise

3 large artichokes
6 loin pork chops, 1-inch thick
  salt and pepper
  flour
1 tablespoon oil
1 1/2 cups sliced onions
1 clove garlic, minced
1 cup beef broth
2 tablespoons wine vinegar
1 bay leaf
1 tablespoon Dijon mustard
1 cup half-and-half

Prepare and cook artichokes as directed for **Whole Artichokes** (see page 9) and cut into quarters. Season chops with salt and pepper; coat with flour. Brown thoroughly on both sides in oil. Remove chops; drain excess fat. Sauté onions and garlic over medium heat until golden. Add broth, vinegar and bay leaf; bring to a boil. Place chops in skillet with artichokes. Bake, covered, at 350° F for 1 hour or until artichokes and

chops are tender; baste occasionally.
Remove artichokes and meat to platter.
Remove bay leaf. Add mustard to pan liquid;
boil until reduced to half. Stir in half-and-half;
simmer until thickened. Salt and pepper to taste.
Serve artichokes and chops with sauce.

Makes 6 servings

Lamb and Bulgur-Filled Artichokes

      water
 1/3 cup bulgur
  2   large California artichokes
 1/4 cup *each* finely chopped onion and
         green bell pepper
  1   tablespoon oil
 3/4 pound ground lamb
 1/2 cup chopped tomato
  2   tablespoons minced parsley
 1/2 teaspoon dried mint, crushed
 1/4 teaspoon salt
 1/8 teaspoon pepper

Pour 1 cup boiling water over bulgur; let stand 1 hour.
Drain well. Prepare and cook artichokes as directed for
Whole Artichokes (see page 9). Sauté onion and green
pepper in oil until tender. Add lamb and cook until lamb
is browned and crumbly; drain excess liquid. Stir in
bulgur, tomato, parsley, mint, salt and pepper. Cook
and stir 1 minute. Halve artichokes lengthwise; remove
center petals and fuzzy centers. Place artichokes in

$8 \times 8 \times 2$-inch glass baking dish; fill
centers with lamb mixture. Pour $\frac{1}{2}$ inch of
water into baking dish. Bake, uncovered, at
$350°$ F about 15 minutes or until filling is
thoroughly heated.

Makes 4 servings

A nutritious staple in the Middle East,
bulgur *consists of wheat kernels that
have been steamed, dried and crushed.*

Chicken Jerusalem

16 to 20 California baby artichokes
1 1/2 pounds chicken breasts, boned,
     skinned and sliced (about 1/4-inch
     thick across the grain)
    salt and pepper
2 tablespoons vegetable oil
1/4 cup sliced celery
1/2 cup sliced mushrooms
1/2 cup dry white wine
1/4 teaspoon *each* dried rosemary and oregano,
     crushed
1/2 cup heavy cream
2 cups hot, cooked white rice

Prepare artichokes as directed for **Baby Artichokes** (see page 11); cut into halves. Season chicken with salt and pepper. Sauté in oil over medium heat about 3 minutes. Add celery, mushrooms and artichokes; sauté 3 to 5 minutes. Add wine, rosemary and oregano; simmer about 2 minutes. Stir in cream and cook until liquid is reduced by half. Season to taste with salt and pepper. Serve over hot rice.

Makes 4 servings

Fettuccine with Artichokes, Parmesan and Sausage

20	California baby artichokes
4	sweet Italian sausages, casings removed and meat crumbled
1	large onion, chopped
2	cloves garlic, minced
1	cup chicken broth
$\frac{1}{2}$	cup dry white wine
12	ounces fettuccine
$\frac{1}{4}$	cup butter *or* margarine, softened
$\frac{1}{4}$	cup freshly grated Parmesan cheese salt and pepper
2	tablespoons chopped parsley

Prepare artichokes as directed for **Baby Artichokes** (see page 11) and cut into quarters. Sauté sausage over moderately high heat until browned. Add onion and garlic; cook over moderate heat, stirring until onion is golden. Add artichokes, broth and wine. Bring to a boil and simmer, covered, 10 to 15 minutes or until artichokes are just tender. Cook uncovered, stirring occasionally, 8 to 10 minutes or until juices have thickened slightly. Keep warm. Cook fettuccine *al dente*; drain. Toss with butter and Parmesan cheese. Salt and pepper to taste. Sprinkle with parsley. Top with artichoke mixture.

Makes 6 servings

Artichokes with Sweet Italian Sausage

8 small California artichokes *or*
    4 medium artichokes
1 pound sweet Italian sausage
1 tablespoon olive oil
1 clove garlic, minced
1/3 cup finely chopped parsley
1/4 cup dry white wine

Prepare artichokes as directed for **Artichoke Hearts** (see page 10); cut into halves. Slice sausage into 1/2-inch pieces. In oiled skillet, brown sausage; drain. Add artichokes. Cover and cook gently about 20 minutes or until almost tender. Add garlic, parsley and wine. Continue cooking, uncovered, until liquid evaporates and artichokes are tender. Serve hot.

Makes 4 servings

Catherine de Medici, daughter of Il Magnifico *Lorenzo de Medici, is alleged to have introduced the artichoke to the French when she married Henry, son of Francis I of France, in 1533. Although there is no historical record, it is doubtful that she had to wait until her coronation in 1547 for her favorite artichoke dishes to be served at court. For not only were they delicious, but artichokes were reputed to have an aphrodisiac effect, a quality that no 16th-century Frenchman would want to miss.*

Pasta with Sautéed Artichokes

2	medium California artichokes
2 to 3	tablespoons olive oil
2	cups sliced mushrooms
1/4	cup dry white wine
1/4	cup thinly sliced green onions
1	teaspoon dried basil, crushed
	salt
8	ounces mostaccioli, cooked, drained and hot
	grated Parmesan cheese
	cracked black pepper

Prepare artichokes as directed for **Artichoke Hearts** (see page 10) and cut into thin wedges. Heat oil in large skillet over medium heat. Add artichoke wedges and mushrooms; cook 2 minutes. Add wine, green onions and basil; simmer, covered, about 5 minutes or until liquid has evaporated and artichokes are tender. Add salt to taste. Serve over hot pasta. Pass Parmesan cheese and cracked pepper.

Makes 4 servings

Cypress Point
Seafood Spectacular

5 large California artichokes
8 ounces medium raw shrimp,
   peeled and deveined
8 ounces bay scallops
$\frac{1}{2}$ cup butter
8 ounces Dungeness crab meat
8 ounces sour cream
1 package (8 ounces) cream cheese
8 ounces shredded Parmesan cheese, *divided*

Prepare and cook artichokes as directed for **Whole Artichokes** (see page 9). In a large saucepan, sauté shrimp and scallops in butter just until shrimp starts to turn pink. Stir in crab, sour cream, cream cheese and $\frac{3}{4}$ of the Parmesan cheese. Cook until heated through, stirring occasionally. Remove center petals and fuzzy centers of cooked artichokes. Fill artichokes with seafood mixture and sprinkle with remaining Parmesan cheese. Place artichokes under hot broiler on middle rack until cheese starts to bubble and brown. Serve immediately.

Makes 5 servings

Conversions

LIQUID

   1 Tbsp = 15 ml
   ½ cup = 4 fl oz = 125 ml
   1 cup = 8 fl oz = 250 ml

DRY

   ¼ cup = 4 Tbsp = 2 oz = 60 g
   1 cup = ½ pound = 8 oz = 250 g

FLOUR

   ½ cup = 60 g
   1 cup = 4 oz = 125g

TEMPERATURE

   400° F = 200° C = gas mark 6
   375° F = 190° C = gas mark 5
   350° F = 175° C = gas mark 4

MISCELLANEOUS

   2 Tbsp butter = 1 oz = 30 g
   1 inch = 2.5 cm
   all-purpose flour = plain flour
   brown sugar = demerara sugar
   heavy cream = double cream